Email Poet: A Mixed Bag New & Old

D.C. Turner

Published by D.C. Turner, 2024.

While every precaution has been taken in the preparation of this book, the publisher assumes no responsibility for errors or omissions, or for damages resulting from the use of the information contained herein.

EMAIL POET: A MIXED BAG NEW & OLD

First edition. July 11, 2024.

Copyright © 2024 D.C. Turner.

ISBN: 979-8218471132

Written by D.C. Turner.

Table of Contents

Preface	1
Darkest Dark of Darkened Darkness	2
An Altered Child	4
When Will It End	6
My Soul Has Turned Pale	8
Lucifer	11
The Candle	12
Blown Across The Reeds	14
Standing Your Storm	15
The Flaw Reverts To You	16
Horrific Shrills	18
A Strange Animal, Indeed!	20
What I Felt Just Then	22
Rhyming With Orange, Maybe	24
Twenty-Four, Soon To Be Twenty-Five	25
Honeysuckle	26
Poetic Life: A New Vision	28
My Epiphany	34
Infinitely Complete	35
Silence	43
Our End	44
Sea of Like-Minded Dreams	45
The Promise	47
A Lonesome Dream	48
A Dreary Night	49
The Next Journey to Come	50
A Most Beautiful Rose	54
The One Beside Me	57
Endless Escape	59
Beauty of My Being	60
Another Moment in Time	61

Captured It, Perfectly	64
Empty Cups and Dreams	65
Regardless	66
Truffles for Our Delight	67
Lost in Your Beauty	69
I Treasure You	70
Your Light	71
Darkness of This Life	72
We Did It	74
A Teardrop Seals My Miss	75
Musical Song	76
A Tale of a Story: Introduction	78
A Tale of a Story: The Kingdoms	80
A Tale of a Story: To Be Considered	82
A Tale of a Story: Crossroads	84
Dream Escape	86
Fifty-Four, Soon to Be Fifty-Five	87
Exit Stage Left	88

Acknowledgments

To my amazing daughters Christy and Samantha, and my wonderful grandchildren Shawn, Lucas, Melody and Sophia. I love you all very much! Also, I want to thank Cynthia Brown (She's always in my heart!) and a very special thanks to my gracious friend, Stacey Watts (Look her up, she's a writer too!). I can share my writings thanks to their encouragements. Thank you most sincerely! I love you all!

Preface

Thank you for taking the time and interest to read my writings. All of which I created out of my life experiences. Some are merely wandering thoughts corralled and gathered together for entertainment. It is with great hope you will find this meager book to be an enjoyable read. Some of my offerings you may have already read in my previous book, Email Poet. I've included some works unpublished in book form, mixed in with writings shared only with those closest to me. The layout is of no particular order, as my life has unfolded in no particular order. Who knew it could be something unpredictable? In reading, may you find something within that resonates with you in a positive way. Enjoy!

D. C. Turner

Darkest Dark of Darkened Darkness

The night is cold, most very still... darkened so.
I travel alone in this darkness of the darkest dark,
But I have a flicker of light that is my flame.

Should you find yourself wandering in the darkest
Dark of darkened darkness and happen to see
A flicker of a light. Come now, you are welcome, for it is me!

'Tis not much of a flame to light much of the way,
But 'tis a flame all the same shedding warmth, I say.
Providing a glimpse of light in the darkest darkness of night

While we walk together, all of nowhere, standing very much still.
For the dark of the darkest darkened night is thick in its frill.
But I have this flicker of light that just might dance for our muse.

To soften the pains of our darkened ways,
That the darkest darkened night does pursue.
It's not much of a flicker to make a flame, but one all the same,

On this night so cold, most very still... darkened so.
It does shed warmth by which to stand, easing our pain.
Watch it dance in happy silence, ecstatic to be alive.

For it knows that in the darkest dark of darkened darkness,
Nothing ever survives to tell of where it is or has been.
But the fact it dances means it's alive and someone is there to share with.

An Altered Child

Early life:

The sun breaks the morn
Ushering in a serene day
Filled with the utmost perfection.

Likewise, a child rises to stand
Observing this new perfected life
Graced upon an unscathed face.

Nothing is more awe inspiring
To this child witnessing fluent
Sounds of peace and harmony...

Transitioning Young Adult:

As the moon waxes the earth,
Clouds begin to appear
With each new day allotted.

Still young in heart and soul,
The now older child hears thunder
Escape the volatile cave of the elder.

Worthlessness creeps
Into the spirit of paradise,
As the sense of self dissipates.

Adulthood:

A familiar horizon breaks the darkness,
But the difference can not be discerned
By the now matured child of yesterday.

Clouds have blotted the sky's blossom.
Warmth of light no longer felt,
As the altered child screams within.

The matured vessel listens
Not to the voice of their inner child,
Only the voice of the addict screaming... feed me.

When Will It End

It is time...
It's not easy for me.
I must see
What I don't want to believe.

It is time...
For me to accept truth.
Move on, another poof!
Dance another foot loose.

Time...
Is at hand
For this man
To understand.

Time...
Is no longer his.
Much undone, missed.
A goodbye kiss.

It is time...
To turn out the light.
Take one last look, so bright.
Leave behind, say good night.

Time...
Never friendly to him.
Moving on, yet again.
Time, when will it end?

My Soul Has Turned Pale

Mother goddess of the moon,
I beg of you, release me
Of my solitude.
Let the solstice have its end.

Father Zeus of the heavenly skies,
Begging your forgiveness, end my pains
Granting me this one wish;
Let a new life be mine to begin.

Hades, what is it you wish of me?
What price must my freedom pay?
Have you not all that I am already?
Where is it my embers so lack to burn?

If no other wish can be granted
To such an abomination, as I,
Then take this heart from my chest.
Feed it to the worms in the pit of decay.

Take my soul, let it feed the dragon's den.
Rip from me, my very essence of being.
Torture me to a rotting core,
Lest I hurt a lifetime more.

God, help me in this plight!
Help me see my way through another night.
Lucifer, oh Lucifer... are you truly friend?
I feel you will be the only one at the end.

I've seen you, your tempting ways.
I am guilty of summoning you on lost days.
Yes, you immediately bid your reply.
How foolish it was of me to even think

A granted wish is without weight.
A burden I requested, and one I so received.
How my ignorance has left my soul to bleed.
Wake me, Mother, from this nightmare.

Let me know I'm not alone, that you are there.
Please, I beg once more of you!
Mother, help me from wherever you are,
To erase these earthly scars.

If my sufferings can not be ceased,
Then take my penance, and pay for another.
Let me be the sacrifice for the sake
To make another lost soul be found.

Take me... I'm lost, anyway.
Help one more worthy than I.
Feed them the grapes of heaven's wine.
Set them a banquet from which to feed.

Give to those who are in need.
I'll gladly take the tax of the cost,
So long as their souls are not lost.
Take my eyes, give to them.

Let them see the errors
Of where I have been.
So, they may learn to steer clear
Of the path I have so beaten.

Should my sufferings save at least one who's lost,
Then I will accept this suffering as not vain.
I'm ready for the tally, the balance of the scale.
For my life, my heart, my soul have turned pale.

Lucifer

I search for love; I find none.
I have paid for love, received none.
Love is elusive to me, hates me.
What is it I do not see?

I have prayed for love. Heaven was closed.
I've used a hound to find love, a broken nose.
Researched, studied, educated in love.
Yet, no matter what... I received none.

My wings are broken. I can not fly.
Love in this heart has completely died.
I loved once, but love ran from me.
A bitterness eventually overcame me.

Who's to say how it entered my heart?
I was not present and had no part.
A light, a magnificent light I did bear.
But that, too, did leave me alone there.

My divine woes, there where I stood,
Was damnation for what I misunderstood.
They became a hanging noose for thee.
Banishing from all of heaven, Lucifer, me.

The Candle

I light a cigarette, taking a break.
Spilling out my mind's abundant produce.
Wondering what you're doing now?

Are you still recording your own journey?
The path you have walked; stumbled; danced?
I look around, seeing what has changed.

Looking out the window, cold; gray.
Rain is coming down like shaken salt.
Are they tears of heaven, ice bulbs?

I wonder how you are; safe, warm, happy?
When will I know, today, tomorrow, ever?
Missing you is an understatement, falling short.

I light a candle to remind me of your dance.
In my mind, I see you, feel you, know you.
Does your candle dance with mine as one?

I peer deep within the candle's flame.
Can you feel me looking, feeling, touching?
Your beauty gives my candle's flame a brilliance.

Does your inspiration feel mine, aspired?
I grab the dance with my hand, swaying, dancing.
Is it your dance the candle portrays, loves?

Setting the flame on the windowsill, displayed,
Snow begins to drift down, eloquent, dancing.
It appears to flock to the window in masses, in love.

Can you feel the warmth of the cold gathered for you?
The candle flame dances brighter, higher, passionately.
I grab the flame once more, holding it in my hand.

Warmth, love, passion I do feel in my light of soul.
I return the flame from where it was taken with love.
A flame is not to be caged, contained, restricted.

Realizing the importance of setting it free, I open the window.
The candle's flame leaps out into the mass of snow.
Will it return, leave the candle alone, leap free?

Snow begins to cry with tears of joy; love,
As the flame graces each flake with a lick.
It leads itself back to its love, the candle.

Blown Across The Reeds

The stardust beckons us to explore, search,
Find what clues are left for us to see...
The ones chosen for such infirmary.

The universe calls our name, our birth,
Our very being begging for us to believe
What has been recorded in the starry sea!

Pleading for us to reach out and touch, feel,
Understand what it means to be heavenly.
Never to let go of the gift given unto you and me.

Come, my Love. Come with me, reel
In all that you see! Reach out freely
Grasp, absorb what is before you, simply be

An investigator of the heavens; our birth right.
You and I, together, shall gather the pieces
Of the puzzle in the cosmos... galactically free!

Let us go, yes, on this most favored of nights.
Exploring the fires of the light in heaven's creed,
With our passes of freedom blown across the reeds!

Standing Your Storm

This is not my script... you hold the pen.
Remember that, when you hear
Me speaking words so softly.
It's the love in this soul you wrought.

With every letter in every word on every line
You write this poetry of heart that is not mine.
It is yours, rightfully so, for you inspire me.
What else is there to being inspired? Nay.

You not only make my life complete,
You've made my life... a living treat.
I bow to you as your servant forever more.
Bidding your command, or standing your storm.

The Flaw Reverts To You

I am imperfect, perfectly flawed.
It matters not what you think you saw.
I am me, nothing more can I be.
Never pretending to be what I am not.
No worrying about what I have or haven't got.
Except, perhaps the lack of one to share with me
All that is called and considered my dreams.

Do I look to be happy or saddened?
Or somewhere in between, maybe?
A tidal wave of ever changing force?
I am, without any doubt or exception,
All of these manifestations of imperfection.
Not in singular form, but all at once.
I am an emotional soup, Tour de France.

So, am I perfect? Yes, to the degree of my flaw.
Just what exactly did you think you saw?
If you must know, look at the book of human traits.
Read it from start to finish.
You'll find me in most every sentence.
I am the one much in need.
The one wearing his tears on the sleeve.

The joker bringing laughs to everyone.

The jester entertaining whoever shall come
Seeking to be entertained by this unique man.
An understanding ear for those of that need.
Encouraging the oppressed souls, that's me!

Comforting the wounded, battle torn hearts.
You'll find me in the pages of "Feelings Torn Apart".
It matters not what or who I am to be.
In your eyes, I will be nothing more than you see.

So, it all depends on the correctness of your vision,
Who you see, what I am to be in your eyes.
Whatever you see, I am certain I can't deny
Being that one. Unless it is a lie that is not true.
Then, of course, the flaw reverts to you.

Horrific Shrills

Placid in appearance, the night stands still.
You listen closely to a horrific shrill.
Want wells up beneath the breast,
As a weakened call manifests.
Appendages turn to run away,
But you find they will only stay.
Quaking muscles fearing the sound
Have, once again, let you down.
Begging in a silent scream
For this to be but a dream,
You realize, your staring eyes
Are affixed to the riverside,
As it rolls on by.
Then suddenly,
Something catches your eye
Taking your mind to another place,
As you see pass by a familiar face!
It's not the horror previously thought,
But a desperate rescue being sought.
Your strength begins to come back, again,
While you quickly turn, ignoring your pain.
Searching in desperate need,
You find right above your knees
A limb just the right size
To rescue the one with scared eyes

From the river's floor once more.
You reach down with a gentle touch,
Picking up the kitten who loves you so much.
Rolling over away from the deep,
You slowly drift back into a placid sleep.

A Strange Animal, Indeed!

There's this animal in Australia.
And I'm here to tell ya
It's the only one of its kind!

I saw it on The Discovery Channel,
And they say it is a mammal.
The weirdest creature, the only one you'll find!

By the information that they give,
It is the only representative
Of its family and genus.

It has a bill just like a duck,
Spurs you don't want to get stuck
With, because it is venomous!

It has the feet of an otter.
Lives mostly in the water,
As it hunts for food each day.

For all that it's worth,
It doesn't give live birth.
Only eggs does it lay!

Here's another fact:
When you look behind its back,
You'll see a beaver-like tail.

Interesting to know,
Should you ever go,
It's the state emblem of New South Wales!

If you ask what I may think,
I'll take some paper and ink,
And sit to draw you a chart.

Cause to me it seems to be,
That our God, so heavenly
Made this thing with leftover parts!

Far enough, I have gone,
The name is what you long.
So, no need for you to fuss.

Sit down in your chair.
I'll tell you loud and clear.
The name of this animal is Platypus!

If you don't believe it's true,
I'll leave it up to you
To research and to read.

As you discover what is known,
And you continue on,
You'll see it is a strange animal, indeed!

What I Felt Just Then

I want to explode... like a nuclear bomb
And release this pressure that's lingering on

Yes, explode... and set free
All these feelings and pain inside of me

I want to explode... like the wrath of God
Releasing the energy of a high voltage rod

I have to explode... it's a reckoning
Of all the things that are wrecking me

To explode... in the universe
Is to go super nova killing the curse

To explode... what's been placed on me
So that maybe I could make someone see

To explode... would let these feelings be gone
All the ways people have done me wrong

I want to explode... out in space
And be a new light shining in the face

Yes, explode... the fuse is lit
And I'll go off in a little bit

I can't explode... I must disarm
To no one do I want to cause any harm

So, I explode... with my pen
And use these words to show the state I'm in

And I explode... these clouds of ink
Perhaps I can get someone to stop and think

Rhyming With Orange, Maybe

I think I've found a way.
Yes, just today,
To rhyme with the word orange!
I'm not sure,
It's quite a blur,
The depth or range
Of the limited use.

Twenty-Four, Soon To Be Twenty-Five

Twenty-four soon, to be twenty-five.
How did I make it this far and survive?
I have traveled near, and traveled far.
Stared at the ground, and gazed at the stars!
The paths I've walked have been smooth and rough.
The hills I've climbed have been easy and tough.
I've fished the waters, with some easy catch.
I've floated a few, where I was no match.
Flying with birds, so ever high.
Crashing down, as they waved goodbye.
I've ridden the horse, oh can't you see?
The horse has too ridden me.
I've run with dogs in a pack,
Ran so far, I barely made it back.
I've run through the jungle and survived...
I'm twenty-four, soon to be twenty-five.

Honeysuckle

Traveling this path, I have many flowers
To remind me of the landscapes I've explored.
Many have withered and dried, leaving only a memory,
But a memory is more beautiful than a thousand flowers.

In my hands, I hold a love that is more powerful
Than all of humanity can imagine it to be.
I hold a power that runs through me with the strength
Of an electrical thunderbolt bolting through the sky.

Yet, I reach out to pluck another flower from the roadside.
It isn't a beautiful rose, as one might expect it to be,
But a simple honeysuckle bearing a sweet nectar
That removes the bitter taste left upon my tongue.

A bitterness left by the thorns bared by so many.
Again, I find renewal in my faith for love, life, humanity.
Yes, I hold a power that reforms lives into wonders
Breaking all barriers of sadness, loathing; hate.

For if in the jungles of life, amidst the tangled vines,
I can find a sweetness that prevails all pricking caused
By the many thorns, then surely I can find forgiveness
In my heart for all the flowers that have withered and dried?

With that being a truth, I have found memories
Serve me best along my travels; journey.
For in my memories, I can choose to avoid
Any thorns that may prick my skin, bringing blood.

Poetic Life: A New Vision

When we speak of life, we speak in terms of use.
It is very tangible, a thing called life.
It has all the characteristics of perishable items.

Time limitations concerning "shelf life".
Variable applications for beneficial use.
In both subjects, we find them.

With that thought in mind, not to be wasted,
Consider one or the other as the other:

The coldness we feel, dislike,
Of another that breaks our hearts.
Is much the same as a perishable blend.

Like the cold preserving our foods,
It, too, will preserve hearts for a later time.
For when we find another, the heart will mend.

With this in thought, hold close in heart
That there is a second, a companion to the cold:

The warmth we feel, and love very much so
Of another, ignites our hearts, our flame,
As much the same as the heat of that we eat.

For our fuel is alive with the fire beneath it.
So, too, is the soul; heart; mind when alive.
To be alive is to be whole; complete.

With these thoughts in your heart, not lost,
Consider a division of balance that is, and will be:

Cold/Warmth.
Hate/Love.
Death/Life.

Cold is absorbed to become warmth.
Hate is not known without love, death without life. Contemplate:

cold = dloc = doc(king) = still/motionless = Ice
warmth = htmraw = heat (ht) (the)m raw = molecules move when excited = out of the rawness of cold we create warmth = Fire (Flame)
hate = etah = tah (acronym) = total abdominal hysterectomy (medical definition) = permanent abortion of life = Death

With some thought, we can extract,
Through the preservation of our coldness:
Warmth dissipates our bitterness of the cold.

This can be seen with the naked eye, literally, spiritually.

Circumvent (definition: - get around restriction: to find a way of avoiding restrictions imposed by a rule or law without actually breaking it.) this formula:

Cold/Warmth = Comfort = Peace
Hate/Love = Comfort = Peace
Peace + Comfort = Love

Love is the reward we seek in our hearts.
Too often, it cannot be contained for being torn apart.
Due to our lack to lend to our hearts, preservation.

Preservation begins in the field.
How we tend our gardens dictates our yields.
This is plain to see without reservation.
But too often, many have hesitations...

In this, we find life is not a singular, but a multiple.
Even single cells are multiples forming a whole; One.
E Pluribus Unum: Out of Many, One

Translated:

E (mathematical constant) = Constant (number theory)
Pluribus (translated - often, frequently) = Pluri (combining form) (Plur from Latin- plus = more, plures = several, many) + Bus (Lat. Omnibus = for all) = Many
Unum = One

No single cell lives singularly, but contrast.
Living in groupings, merging, growing together

Forming what we know as life (humanity), a life (you).

Another thought to keep in mind; analyze.
Consider the possibility before our eyes:

Constant/Many = Generations
Generation = One

Preservation of our hesitations,
Before us, repeating now, to come in generations.
A cycle was born unto us all.
We must break it, preventing fall.

The answers are amongst us.

In each is a piece to add to our cause.
Our cause is a machine of great stopping power.

Let each flame shed light on the work at hand.
Lighting a nut or bolt to hold firm a new manufacture.
Seeing that all is not lost on future's accord.

To know is to be intimate in knowledge of another.
Let us know our errors, correcting them with knowledge.
For if a mistake is knowingly acknowledged,
It stands to not be repeated, or folie (psychiatry - a psychological disorder of thought or emotion; a more neutral term than mental illness)

In all this, we come back to our manufacture of our perishables.
The cold that preserves for our future use.
The warmth to delight our senses, make use of.

Trace back to manufacturer, consider:

Manufacture = Manuf(r)acture = Man you fracture

If our manufacture is true, and correct.
Our Cold is dissipated by the Warmth of our flame.

Our perishable is preserved from Death, flourishing

In the light of day, lighting the darkness.
Filling us with Love, Comfort, with Peace.
Taking Life, giving Life, living Life.

We hereby extract:

Death = htead = head = our spirit = we choose = Extinguished
Love = evole = evolve = evolution = cylces = Revolution
Comfort = trofmoc (acronym) = Taking Role of Mother of Creation
Peace = ecaep (acronym) Early Childhood Education and Assistance = parenting = teaching = Success
Life = efil (acronym) = European Federation for Intercultural Learning [variation = e(i)f(f)el tower = your tower] = being receptive/acceptive = Burning

So, as in death, our folie is not repeated,
But our Love is spread like sunflowers in a field.
Knowledge that lasts for many generations.

A passing of a different kind, death becomes life.
Whereby the cycle is broken and reversed.

A star is a star, is a ball of gathered flame.
Let your star go nova, filling you with light.
Let it be a supernova, passing your flame.
Spreading the warmth of new life.

Nova - *n.* a star that ejects some of its material in the form of a cloud and becomes more luminous in the process

Supernova = A rare celestial phenomenon involving the explosion of most of the material in a star, resulting in an extremely bright, short-lived object that emits vast amounts of energy.

My Epiphany

Holy Crap!
What is that?
Is that what I think I see?
Surely not? I can't believe!

Just like a rat,
That is fat,
It snuck in on me.
Carrying, as a rat does a flea,

A customized message.
An utterly refined presage
Telling the fool I am to be.
It is, undeniably, my epiphany.

Infinitely Complete

What does the night hold? I don't know.
I have misplaced my use of know.

What will tomorrow bring? Know I not.
How can I? It's something I've yet, forgot.

What is my future to be? I have no clue.
Is seeing my pains, what I really want to do?

Why is happy so afraid of me? Do what?
It's fearing of happy in me, that I do wrought.

How will I know what I want will last? Give me a break!
I won't, long as I'm living in memory's mirror, make no mistake.

Why do all my quests so willfully fail, erupt? No, I have it wrong.
I'm a successful master of self destruct, skillfully leaving a trail, realm of gone..

What is it I keep doing, but never right? Who am I trying to convince?
Look back at all my writes. Can I see the success at which I wince?

Surely, I can accept being only human? Of course I can, can't I?
I know I'm no Paul Newman, I'm only me. But just what is that? Who am I?

I make no sense yet, the most sense of all. I am my worst enemy.
So, it only makes sense to issue apologies to all for exposing what is in me.

Is this demon ever going to leave? Not if I don't make him go.
Time is nothing of importance, see? Leave, demon! I, you no longer know!

Now, can I make an unusual turn? How do I know? It's uncommon for me.
Yes, I can! That much I've learned! Go for it! Let my pen fly free!

I'm a person of happen stance. Living in a world of perception plants. No one seems to understand anything about me, this man. I have been here on this planet since what seems like the beginning of time. True, if you count the beginning as the initial firing of my mind. I've always questioned every rule that has ever been interjected into my life. But most especially concerning all my emotionally reflective poems, who's to tell me what I feel, if it's wrong or right? After all, it is my life I write. Right? Right! I shy away from so many complimentary words given to me by so many others that it's not funny. It's a problem that is incendiary within me, firing to a crisp. Internally I smother. All due to a simple fact. My self worth was stolen from me when I was very young, and never given back... Enough with me, for there is so much more in this world to see!

Have you ever noticed the trees growing on a daily basis? Or noticed the frowns on so many faces, in so many different places? There's a reason for the tree growing so slowly, and there's a reason for all those frowns. Reasons we don't know. Have you ever seen God working in real time in your life? If you don't believe in God, that's alright. He still believes in you! That's all you need Him to do. Slow down in your crazy world, take your time looking around to observe. All the answers to our questions of why can be found here with us beneath the sky! No need to disturb our Lord. He left the answers with us, so we would not get bored. My, my, my, what a welcomed surprise! It's all right here in front of our eyes! Have you ever noticed in the middle of your complaints that someone is knocking on your door bearing problems that would make you faint? I've had that to happen, just this very day. He claimed it was an accident, apologizing it all away. I told him the first time he might not understand. But when God uses rhyme talking to this man, it is never on deaf ears His words fall upon. I see Him every time. Then the same thing happened not an hour later, maybe less than half. He sent the same one to me, in the hope we both would grasp. The power of a being who loves us so completely laid His body on a cross to be nailed in wrists and feet. Not for the sake of control, as we are so carefully lead. But to prove He gave to us the same and very power He used to defeat death! Never have I claimed to be Christian, I am way too much of the weak. I'm nothing but a sinner at best. This is what I speak. But the message being sent to me, concerning my complaints. I pointed out to Singapore I had none to be rather quaint.

After he told me how his country is surrounded by so much mortal death. Including his tale of recent homelessness, reduction of his work, and how he is still blessed. With a few of what I call angels, delivering him from defeat to a certain salvation. Now that is when I had to say to him, without hesitation you may not understand what is going on, but I do. He is doing what He does best, humbling me, and you.

Moving on to more interesting facts in life. Do you ever consider by who's measure you are defining wrong and right? Just as a clock ticks and the hands move, even at night. That maybe our sense of time got us in this plight? Have you listened to the words sung by Seal, in the love song Kissed By A Rose? Is that how deep your love goes for the one you love? It should be, should be all you think of. How

about Truly, Madly, Deeply by Savage Garden? The same applies there, too. Words whose caliber are
of the same margin.

How many times has someone asked you or even asked of another by you how do you write so well? Only to find a stumbling block of sophisticated sounding words we know sells? It's not as complicated as one thinks. If it is from your heart, and not from the ratings game, the higher ups tend upon our minds to paint. If you write from the heart, and not from your mind, you'll find it reaches the hearts of readers, every time. Never be afraid to feel and be real. It's the only thing we have of our own. Our thoughts, our mind. What we feel, our hearts. This is where we are strong. Take all your years of hurt and pains. All your memories of yesterday's shame. Put It all in writing, I don't care if it's code. Just write it down, no lying. You'll be thankful, wondering why you never traveled that road. Let the music flow through your veins, open your mind with a new zipper, absorbing all the energies. Energize your mind with the positive vibes. Most importantly, let love find your heart, taking up long-term residence from the start!

Look not only at the river the next time you watch it flow, but look in the river. What you may see, no one ever knows. Will it be your dreams? Maybe. Will it be love? If on your knees, asking please! It can be a white dove, all of this is what it can be. Open your eyes, see more than what you want to see! It's a perfect imperfection that we live! Enjoy all its offerings that it gives!

Break the rules, as you see fit.
Not adhering, some don't get.
Just remember this:
How you see life's gifts
rehtona ot siht ekil kool yaM

It's the folly of perception,

that
always makes
question us to

rules LIKE rulers, of definition
ot
all who keep up with missions

Understand that rules, like rulers, rulers
Do break and get replaced.
Certain ones dictate to each a rule of interest, only to them. But it is by another one's blood that the bill is paid. Who rules? Why were they chosen? What do they do that is so special, aside from being filled with vast knowledge from the point of birth to the day they are convinced they have divinely given worth? I believe I have that worth. Do you believe that? How so? Why? What makes your belief grow? How much do we really know? I know a lot, but less deducting what I forgot! "It's not what you've got, but what you give. Not the life you choose, but the life you live" Lyrics from the song What You Give by Tesla. Yes, I'm within my permissive boundaries (aka rules) y'all, of the copyright

infringement laws! Check it out, if you disagree. Don't take my word for it, disbelieve! Fight that temptation to lean on another one's revelation! Prove me wrong, prove me right. I care not which you prove. Just get out there in life, research for yourself. Find the truth upon all your world's shelves. In the wastebasket of time, anywhere is fine. Just do it for yourselves. After all, that's how the powers came to be. Gaining the trust of you, and of me. To allow them to "Take care of our needs".

If you're still with me, made it this far
I'll try to close this a little less bizarre.
Slow down in your life's car.

Notice what you're missing.

Life is too fast, as it is, my friends
Pushing the pedal too fast causes wheels to spin.
Let nature absorb into you once again.
The sky is reaching out with a kiss.

Can't you see the sun trying to comfort you?
Lending its warmth, its sustenance for food?
A living god unknown amongst what we choose.
Ignored by "Rulers" and labeled Pagan.

Do Re Mi is there a god here, I spy?
I do believe it's in the songs we buy.
Reduced in rank, forced within our minds
By those wishing us to believe what they say, again.

My friends, all I try to get you to see
Is pay attention to your pets, your trees.
Phenomenon is more than just a movie to see,

It's: an observable fact or event

Open your minds, take back ownership
Of what is a birthright, not leader whipped.

It's all that you have, coupled with your heartbeat.

It's your duty to keep them as one, infinitely complete.

Silence

With the touch of a finger
Upon the midnight air,
A lone star once cradled
Disappears beneath dreams
Whispered deep inside
A faint, rhythmic heartbeat.
Waiting alone in silence...

Our End

Was it not a light in darkness
That gave sight to these barren eyes,
Seeing nothing more than deserted plains,
Filled with mounds of wilted life wasted away?

Did not that same light encourage hope
Within a hopeless soul, allowing it to find a promise
In a brighter tomorrow, cresting a fiery horizon,
If given the proper time for manifestation?

Behold! Here is testament to that very light.
A light that shines upon each of our souls daily.
Behind every dark cloud, every drop of rain,
Light does work towards our salvation... if not our end.

Sea of Like-Minded Dreams

Kiss me with your rosebud lips.
Move me with your swaying hips.
Love me with your beating heart.
Inspire me with that very part...

Feed my flame the nectar of your fruit.
Entice my senses with your flowered bloom.
Pull me closer with your radiant hair.
Hypnotize me with your cranial stare...

Close my eyes with your hush.
Open my mind to your pleasant lush.
Embrace my being with your very soul.
Lead me into my age, as I grow old...

Take my hand, let me show you me.
Follow me to the land of make believe.
Let me show you how real it can be when love is fair.
Show me with all you are, just how much you care...

Let us inspire each other to love deeper.
Being our own sworn swan song keepers.
Encourage me to dance your dance of dances,

As I encourage you to open up to life's entrances...

Follow me not, do not lead.
Be my soul's counter balancing me.
Reach to the stars with a gentle touch,
Plucking what we need, just enough...

Envelope me in your sin.
I will surely come back again, and again.
Pull me tight upon your breast.
Fill me with your inner zest...

Harness the Milky Way, the love of God.
Unleash it on me, I affirm with a nod.
Take me, as I take you; meld with me.
Let us be free in our sea of like-minded dreams...

The Promise

It's the dream that never ends...
Weaving in and out of every thought,
Taking away all the emptiness of today.

It's the promise that never wins...
Painting illustrious tapestries
Upon the mind, so easily swayed.

It's the artistry, clearly within...
All the tears and pain
Felt inside, escaping through wordplay.

It's the song never penned...
Only expressed through sound,
Releasing those feelings stored away.

In the end, it's a dream...
Of a promise which is never kept,
Making it through another day.

A Lonesome Dream

In the mind a lonesome dream
Wanders amidst sparkled skies.
Deep within the vast emptiness
Of darkness between the lights.

Searching for warmth dreamt
Of so many times amongst turbulent
Air filled with cloudiness, undefined.

Shivering against the glistening rain,
Falling far away from stars
Bereft of light, lingering on.

Long forgotten, long since faded away
Into the darkness of night,
Only to become a dream
Kept within a forgotten soul.

A Dreary Night

Was it not a dreary night that came down upon my soul, stealing away the slightest ray of hope my spirit possessed? Did not a fire manifest rekindling a smoldering ache within this heart of darkness, igniting an unquenched pain to last evermore? Was it not your breath that blew fervent winds upon my ear, reaching deep within the concave of my being, destroying the very foundation upon which I stood? Did you not place dew drops of rain upon the globes of my vision to roll free from this heart? Did you not condemn my very existence? Is not damnation the gift you gave unto me to keep for all of eternity?

I'm left with only questions for which I already know the answers. Borrowed is this life I possess. I defer my digression in the heart; soul; mind; spirit. In its place, I gather kindling to reignite what shall become a new fire of hope for salvaging what is left of all that I am; my life. I long to correct the errors I've made along the path of my journey. I long to live as, what is perceived to be, a normal human being...

The Next Journey to Come

I was sitting while smoking my pipe,
Contemplating the recent past.
Revisiting pleasant moments, words, you.

As I took a gentle aromatic draw,
It occurred to me that time could have been
Much different. Sad, lonely; without you.

Then I saw a story unfold before my eyes.
A story that told more than just any story.
It showed me now and Zen.

Not of the Led Zeppelin variety, but of propriety
To my mind, and mine alone.
It was a story of myself, solitary, afraid; has been.

As I sat back, taking it all in like a motion picture,
A great clock appeared right in front of me.
Real as time itself. No dials, no record, no sound.

Just a face with numbers, and a pendulum.
The pendulum swung back and forth in silence.
Time was indiscernible, with no indicators.

Just as I was about to think that no sense was being made,
I realized that nothing but sense was manifesting before my eyes.
More than I have ever known at once.

In my whirlwind of a thought, I had treated time
As though it had been flying; running out,
Acting in similar ways of one who is desperate.

Immediately forming haste, anxiety, and foolishness.
I have been foolish many times over.
I suspect I will do so in the future, if not today.

In my haste, I wasted even more pleasant moments.
I sincerely regret this. Completely. Soulfully...
My deepest apologies for that negligence.

Then, as fast as the clock appeared, it changed
Into another story. One before me, yet after, as well.
One where two people, man and woman, are together.

Indications suggested they had been for quite some time.
That occasionally he would depart for a length of time.
She was not too fond of being alone during that period.

She, too, made her own haste. I could relate.
I felt the aches, pains, bitterness; fear of 'alone'.
I wanted to help her, but was forbidden to acknowledge myself.

Then I saw a dragon manifest, devouring all that was around.
The inscription 'Death becomes I, for I am Death' adorned its chest.
I trembled at this site, for I saw my face within.

This dragon had needles sticking out abundantly
Over its entire structure. Broken hearts around its neck.
Destroying all it touched, or even came close to.

By this time, I was in need of more tobacco,
But couldn't let go of the sight before me, as it was
Too horrifying and intriguing, like a film or book.

Next I saw a being, indescribable, except to say alive.
Best described, it had a familiar form, but no form at all.
Ever changing. Very much like modeling clay in raw form.

I had a comfortable sense that this could be most anyone.
It was attempting and reattempting form, but never quite taking form.
I felt as though it was myself beneath a blanket of suffocating clay.

But I had no fear of this sight, nothing of a negative thought about it.
Quite the opposite, in fact. I had a positive sense of form would be found.
This being would become one with understanding and form.

Second nature to all things of understanding. A masterful
Form propagator. He disappeared in a flinch of my eye.
No trace of him. Just gone. But my mind had captured his form.

Now as I reload my pipe, as I did at the beginning,
I am contemplating this ponder of wonder.
One with all seriousness of thought and soul.

I am now making much sense out of this series of entranced
Optical displays before my eye's thoughts.

I have a much more comforting and easy feeling.

A sense of well-being, no matter the length of my presence.
That all has not been in vain, or lost upon uselessness,
Realizing that even a fool is a jester of much learned knowledge.

That time has many faces equal to no time, as we know it.
Our time perceptions are failed, at best. We place the wrong
Value in the right circumstances, and all values in the worst.

Appreciation is a living entity that takes place in the present,
As well as later, to be recalled many times,
Refining our appreciation of being; seeing; living.

That our dragons only devour us when we hide from ourselves.
For the very place we hide within is our dragon's lair.
It devours effortlessly, for we do all the preparations.

We are but raw clumps of clay in a state of constant forming,
No matter how many times we are content to have form.
Change blows in, reforming our lives. With or without consent.

In the end, our molded form is not of a mold, but of soul.
It is an outer reflection of what lies within. We cannot hide
The truth, but one lifetime. Not even the whole of that.

Our heart is what matters for all of eternity and for always.
It is the keeper of our soul, and with that, who we are.
Do you want to take your heart into the next journey to come?

A Most Beautiful Rose

I saw you in your garden, some time back.
Right there, with all those beautiful flowers.
I stood there watching, admiring you so much.
Longing grew in my heart for your presence.

As the people stopped to purchase each beauty,
I wondered why they paid no attention to you.
How could they not see your glory amongst all that was there?
It baffled me, as to the blindness I was witnessing.

But it pleased me all the same, knowing you were there.
I went home, as it was evenings end,
Returning each day for many days after
To witness your beauty in bloom.

Nothing could I find more pleasing to the eye or my soul.
You, my love, are the pinnacle of beauty in these eyes.
Still, I noticed you were being overlooked by those
Who stopped in. Still, I could not understand.

Then it occurred to me what was happening.
All those people saw the beauty of the day.
They wanted and desired that instant beauty.
I, too, appreciated as much.

But their failings came by way of ignorance,
Not knowing that beauty would fall away in haste.
Unaware of the brief life their beauty would afford.
As for me, I knew better of the truth.

Whereas they were seeing the flowers in bloom,
I saw you, your beauty surviving the test of time.
You outshine all the other flowers, my Love.
Your bloom may have been less at the time,

But I am certain that all those who passed before,
Would repent, today of their error.
They could not see what I saw.
In you, I saw your heart, your love.

Now, when visitors come to indulge me,
It is never a failing to hear of your beauty.
Proud I am, I must say when I hear those words.
For they know not what was before.

You were withered, drooping, and sad, to say the least.
Heartbroken, your will no longer willing.
All you wished for was a ray of warmth
And shine from the sun, a little refreshing of water.

You longed for a gentle touch; kindness in voice
To be vibrated in the air for your ears to be soothed.
Encouragement from the heart to be shared with your heart.
Sufficient room to breathe, to see the world around you.

To know that you are alive, wanted, desired; loved.
Praises to acknowledge your accomplishment.
What those didn't know then, now see today.
You, my love, are a most beautiful rose.

The One Beside Me

In the house of words, I cannot speak.
Barely able to stand on my feet.
Taken aback by the one in front of me.
Oh, the wondrous beauty I do see!

My heart yells up into my ears,
Thump, thump, thump, as I peer,
Saying, "Go speak to her, acknowledge a star.
Let her know just who you are."

But my throat is of a constricted mess,
Choking back all of this nervousness.
I reach and grab a story renown,
Trying to implicate to her my own.

"Beauty and The Beast," ...
I drop it... How clumsy of me.
Embarrassment, now I am served.
An awkward situation, to be sure.

Glancing out the of corner of my eye,
I find, to my complete surprise,
She is smiling a lovely smile,
As she glances down my aisle.

Noticing not, I have seen her shine,
I discreetly return to her, mine.
Picking up what was dropped,
I place it back on the top.

Reaching for another known fable,
I walk back towards the table
Feeling a bit more confident.
The time for the walk is well spent.

Gathering what I can with my eye,
I feel a swelling of my pride.
She is to be the one of my life,
Becoming what will be known as my wife.

This I feel deep in my heart,
As I sit to begin my new life's start.
Waking up, I feel it was but a dream.
Until I look at the one beside me.

Endless Escape

Licorice strips glistening
With ruby-diamond drops,
Divided by lemon strings
Over vast seas of cotton swabs.

Mint-sprinkled fudge sticks
Standing in many a row,
As sparklers rise quickly,
Into heaven's throw.

Whispered zinging curtails
Buzzing through the air.
Many thoughts of wonderment
Flow beneath this hair.

Destinations unknown,
Riding within this mind.
It's just another metaphor
Escaping in this rhyme.

Beauty of My Being

I do not know who I am
Or what I am, in my way of seeing.
But, maybe, that's the beauty of my being.

Another Moment in Time

Another moment in time. Another pill, drink, whatever it was… Does it matter what a restless soul would take to assist with their state of relaxation? What matters, however, is it helps to comfort the chilled darkness of night placed upon the skin, though it's a complete falsehood. It also brings a false warmth, convincing enough to allow for a much needed moment of rest; peace. However long that period should last, a minute is a lifetime in a life with no rest.

Perhaps instead of warmth, it's a welcomed numbness that spreads across the soul? Neither does it matter which one it is to be. The end result is what's coveted. Does not a dream come to life within the confines of the restful mind, lest it become a waking nightmare for the restless? A weary soul is poor kindling for a fire soaked in unsettled regret. No embers will ever sparkle their way to the heavens, taking their place amongst the stars, when doused with any regrets aforementioned. An impossibility it most certainly will be.

The next moment arrives, giving no consideration for the previous tranquil moment so desired. It brings with it another cold weight riding on its back, restoring the chill that became so familiar long ago. Too long ago. Too familiar. A soul needs rest, and rest needs a weary soul to justify its existence. What use does existence have for the soul if it's denied the sustenance provided by rest? As it is, a bridle abides the dark's command to fasten itself upon the condemned soul suffering this damnation, while listening to unknown howls echoing throughout the dismal night's wane. Or is it only the sound of the many ponders in mind, flowing as fluent as the broadest rivers descending from the highest mountains of time? Again, it matters not to which it may be. What matters is the constant pull that anchors the soul to the darkness, overshadowing every precious moment of tranquility. A battle lost before it even begins, for a bridle holds fast and strong.

And it is at that moment time enters, showing its aggressive and merciless temperament. Its patience for overcoming the most resistant soul. Is it not the nature of time to spin around, returning every hour from which it was taken to its appointed seat? Time has no conscience to be governed by, quite the opposite. It possesses the greatest ability to ignore all manners of emotion; sufferings. It also possesses a most peculiar ability to slow itself while in the presence of chaos; calamity and moments of complete terror, while accelerating readily, away from the most gratuitous moments filled with much joy, peace, and moments of the utmost euphoric happenings. But all things aside, it's nothing more, and shall always be, just another moment in time.

Captured It, Perfectly

I sat here staring at this blank page,
Trying to find words that perfectly
Capture the feeling of being alone.
Then I realized the page
Has already captured it, perfectly.

Empty Cups and Dreams

What is the prize of an effort that is lost?
Is it a dream destined to ride with Charon,
As he fulfills his role commanded by Hades?

What is a dream without an effort afforded it?
It, surely, is no more than a sail torn
With rips among other flaws within a ship.

What is an effort denied a dream?
Certainly, it must be an empty cup
Clouding the mind, baring no prize.

How can one find hope and inspiration
Within a ship stripped of sails,
Littered with empty cups and dreams?

Regardless

Today, I have to live with the fool I made myself to be yesterday.
But that's okay. I'll make it through the day. Regardless.

Today, I must take care not to repeat yesterday, in no way.
That's okay, too. I will make it through alright. Regardless.

Today, I must be mindful of tomorrow, as I am on this day.
It's okay, I can do that without thought or concern. Regardless.

Today, I must do my best to correct yesterday's wrongs.
I'm okay. I will make it through with flying colors. Regardless.

Today, I must remember to acknowledge all who love me.
We're okay. They know I love them as much as any. Regardless.

Today, I am here alone because of yesterday; what I did.
That's okay, my shadow is still here with me. Regardless.

Today is a day I will repair all that makes me wrong.
It's not okay. I remember doing this yesterday… Regardless.

Truffles for Our Delight

Come, leave your shrinking violet.
Let us probe what lurks within,
Prescribing salves for our wounds.

Seize the moment of our embrace,
Holding close the belle of our pith.
Take me into the crux of your being.

Relish the illumination afforded us.
Take to heart what you feel within.
Amuse your delights against my skin.

Lunar radiance soaks upon our necks,
Exciting our motion alongside the sea's
Mountainous waves of passion.

It is ours, Love, to be had on this eve.
Beckon, the call of the wild; our nature.
Release your demure upon my stroke.

Shh... listen to my heartbeat with yours.
Let us savor every fluff of our touch,
Knowing it is but a moment in time.

Reach in, melding your soul with mine.
Joining flame to flame, inspiring emotion.
Let our moment be truffles for our delight.

Lost in Your Beauty

If I only had three words to describe you,
What three words would I choose?
You are beautiful.

Three words to choose
To describe the heart in you:
It is beautiful.

If that weren't enough to describe you,
What words would I choose?
A beautiful soul.

If I had only one word to describe
When you are not in my life,
Lost.

One word to describe each night we part ways,
Every time our goodbyes we say:
Sad.

What I'd tell anyone, should they ask,
With minimal words, no light to bask:
I am lost in your beauty.

I Treasure You

You are the white that holds the dark of the eye.
The pigment that gives color, washing the gray,
Turning the darkness into a wondrous light.
I treasure you...

You are the seed that makes an apple complete.
The red showcasing passion; its loving way,
Keeping safe deep in your heart of one so weak.
I treasure you...

You are the invisible that holds the stars in the sky.
Letting all shine through, displaying their flame.
So others may see them, each and every night.
I treasure you...

God has set forth a definition for peace, my Love.
Passion was in His heart when He made you.
Yes, I am most certain of all this because
I treasure you...

Your Light

If you, or anyone, ever forget what "light" is,
Or more to the point, your light.
Take a matchstick in a dim-lit room,
Strike it, holding it with the match-head pointing up.
Watch it closely; witness the brilliance it lends.
The energy and power it possesses.
The dance it dances in celebration of its life.
Then you'll have a piece of the image that is your light;
The purpose it lends to the world it lives in…

Darkness of This Life

Looking across the emerald blankets,
As they touch, the clarity of depths unexplored,
I see a reflection of duality kissing the day of night.
My reflection is not present in what is unfolding before my eyes...

I reach out, touching the breath exhaled by the sky.
Could this be God's breath I feel upon my fingertip?
Or, is it the breath of the one I love so dear, riding
Winds of change to inform me I am no longer her desire?

I turn to walk away, reflecting thoughts of brilliance
Once echoed in my heart's mind, stilling turbulent motions.
I feel a tempest is at work to destroy what has become whole.
Distance is being administered by the same one holding my heart.

I take a deep breath of nature's essence, exhaling slowly
With a controlled sigh of uncertainty, fighting back pain's way.
I feel the air beneath the bee's wings as they approach my peace,
Preparing to sting at their earliest want of such inflictions.

I leave the beauty of the inlet's bay, walking
Towards the next sunrise, in anticipation it will rise again.
The moon is awakening to keep the darkness of night at bay.
Will the sun rise as sure as it's setting on me tonight?

I close my eyes to absorb this fantasy that is within,
Recalling the life I hold so dear, the life with her; she is my fantasy.
Another stretch of silence overtaking the sweet music she played
Upon my ear, my soul, my very being of yearn and want.

Is this another endless test of endless testing of my character?
My character has spoken many times over; not one word or action
Has changed, or has it my dearest Love, for whom I take each breath?
Life makes final what is made temporary from the first branching of cells...

No longer do I bath in the breast of life's finest milk to be suckled.
I stand close to the fervent heat of nature's heartbeat atop the cauldron,
Seeking sustenance to further my dream's vision of tomorrow, today.
My dreams are all that I have to carry me through the darkness of this life...

We Did It

Often we hear the question,
"What's wrong with the world?"
We are...

The next time you feel the need to ask,
"What is wrong?" with another remember,
We are...

When you see a familiar pain,
A pain in the heart, remember
We did it...

As you deny having contributed
A wrong trespassing a soul remember,
We all did it...

A Teardrop Seals My Miss

I write these words of heart, missing you.
The love you give me is so pure, so true.
Wanting to touch you once again,
Begging for mercy to be my friend.
Pleading to God, let me hold you just once.
But all I have are these words to share.
I rub them with a softened finger,
As your picture lingers in my mind.
I lift to leave you a kiss,
While a tear drop seals my miss.

Musical Song

Why? You ask why. Have you not been out in the world? Do you not know of it, as I do? Have you not seen the carnage laying before you for all to see? The destitution, desolation and destruction left in humankind's wake? Yet, you ask why. You ask as though you have no eyes by which to see a great and horrendous world filled with atrocities greater than the mind can comprehend. The soul is burdened to carry the weight of such knowledge, should that very knowledge be acquired. Never will it be free from such horrors again. I can only offer you an answer that will fit inside the confines of your innocent mind. Look at the mountains, the seaside, up to the heavens above. Take note of all the colorful flowers on display. Pay close attention to the many shades of blue in our skies, as they fade to black velvet dazzled with fiery sprinkles. Appreciate the preserving nature of the snow-caps on mountaintops untouched by any living thing. Pray you see nothing less than the beauty presented to you, protecting you from the demonic ways of human nature. Humans are the eternal plague cast about the universe, destine to destroy all they touch. And most things beautiful are nothing more than fatal objects designed to either warn us or lure us into their deadly snare. But sometimes, a beautiful thing comes along, reaching past all physical existence and superficial philosophies, grabbing one by the soul to comfort in a way that is unexplainable and inextricably immutable. The cosmos universally knows it as a band of frequencies. Humans call it music.

Music can help a wounded soul through some very hard times. Its invocation can immediately stir powerful emotions from deep within. Or, it can evoke emotional experiences built layer by layer over time. Either way, when it hits true, there's no denying it is there, deep inside the vibrations of your soul. A subtle way we know this is true is by the way the hair on our arms stands up when we resonate with any given score of music or song. It's known as the goose-bump factor. All things being said, the greatest joy I've ever known is equal only to the greatest pain I've ever known. Both being given the name of love. Both being captured in musical song.

A Tale of a Story: Introduction

Where do I begin this story I wish to tell you? Tradition would have it to start at the beginning, but that will not do here. The beginning has little relevance in this uniquely common tale. While the middle only has part of the vital information you need to know. Things I will describe to you. The end? Frankly, the end bypasses the story altogether. And this makes it a moot point even telling the story. I believe the beginning of this story lies somewhere between the traditional starting point and the middle grounds of what will be a fine story, indeed.

It all begins long after all that culminated in the beginning, forming the middle story. But years before the middle came into existence. As with all things, stories and beings alike, there is the usual and most common conception of what is to be. And as we all know, that gives way to birth. Now, here we find nothing unusual or out of the ordinary with the circumstances surrounding growth. But what we find instead is an abnormal essence embedded within the creation itself. An essence that intrigues the listener most especially. Rendering them defenseless against turning away. Indeed, some describe it as being hooked. For the listener is most eager to discover what happens in this tale of events. Yes. All stories are mysterious by the very nature of what is unknown. And thus far, unknown is this story. So, it would be safe to state and assume that we are in the pre-middle age of this tale. Where many things have happened, not worthy of noting, at least concerning the time beforehand. Now, you may ask yourself where this is going and just what is this story about? I'll tell you, but be patient, dear listener. All good things come in time. And time is the very thing we are considering at this crucial point in what will unfold to be a tale of a story.

A Tale of a Story: The Kingdoms

As you are already aware, our story begins long after its conception and birth. It is somewhere just prior to the middle ages of its growth. Obviously, it has a beginning, but little worthiness for mentioning. To be blunt, very common and plain. So let us begin this common and most usual story, being ironically unusual in its very nature, with where it begins, but is not in itself the traditional beginning of a usual and common story.

King Gregory was a ruler of great stature, as great as any that ruled before him in all the lands recorded throughout known history. All the subjects of Livingwell loved their king. He was a fair and just ruler. One who understood he had nothing without the hard work and contributions his subjects afforded. And he showed his gratitude in different ways, ensuring each was never in want of simple necessities, such as food and the like. No kingdom had a greater care for the citizenry of the people. Gregory was the only ruler known in recorded history who ever walked amongst his people alone, without guard and without fear of his loyal subjects. He was a great ruler and very much loved.

King Damon was a rivaling ruler over the land of Darkstone and an immediate threat to the kingdom of Livingwell. All the people feared the wrath and war known to be administered by the Darkstone warriors. Humanity quaked at the mere thought of such war being raged upon their souls. Those warriors had no morals or nobility in any portion of their existence. Many believed that the earth had unleashed hell, releasing all demons and devil hounds from the underworld. I would favor this belief, for no human could ever be so evil and cold as those warriors were. There was a justifiable reason for their fears.

Damon loathed Gregory. He couldn't understand how the subjects of Livingwell loved their ruler so without the strong-arm of rule or fear of punishment. How could a kingdom love their king, giving him all support through their very own will without demonstrable laws and enforcement of those laws? Surely, in his mind, they would eventually turn on their king and the rest of the known world.

He saw this notion to be a plague of the people that would spell certain doom for humanity. This new idea of freewill simply wouldn't work. It would destroy all life and hierarchy, as everyone knew it. The very rulers of all the lands would suffer at the hand of this new disease. It had to be stopped at any cost.

King Damon had much experience with this kind of defiance. He would force his peasant subjects to take part and support his efforts. If they would not do so willingly, he would make them suffer for their refusal and rebellion. He knew how to keep citizens of the kingdom in line, as any ruler knew to be a successful formula for superiority. And the crown was most certainly superior to any peasantry. He was more than prepared to put a stop to a free-living society that threatened to destroy this perfect formulation of rule. A society perceptively without common rule that would undoubtedly turn on themselves and spread like the black plague across the lands, destroying all. Yes, he had a firm resolve to eliminate this newly formed disease.

A Tale of a Story: To Be Considered

Thus far in our tale, we've come to a crucial point. An unordinary point of importance. The listener might perceive, and most certainly would appear to anyone listening, that vital information has not been revealed. Information concerning things farther back towards the beginning, as traditionally observed. Ordinarily, and most commonly, this would be true. But for the sake of our tale, it is not pertinent concerning what is to come. By all means, what came before is of no importance worthy of mentioning. Not at all. The important thing that has not been revealed, which we will discover in just a bit, is what matters. But first, we must consider all the things that have taken place before now. For we are quickly approaching the middle age of our tale, and we know that this is when the most crucial transformation takes place. One in which is the most common of common amongst tales.

Our tale is about to mature into an extraordinary story. We all know this growing spurt happens quite rapidly. It is at this point, in a tale that the beginning has become a moot point no longer fixated within our mind's eye. We have gathered enough information to make sense of what has happened and to intrigue the listener, making them yearn to learn what will come next. Each of these signs are earmarks of a quality tale possessing the fine tenants elevating it into a wondrous story. This is no different, my dear listeners. What is to follow will be of an intriguing quality, taking our tale in many directions. But never back whence it came from. For we have well established the beginning is no longer of any use for our soon-to-be-born-story, as our tale gives birth to it. Let us now explore further into many discoveries awaiting our devoted attention.

As we continue on with our tale giving birth and credentials rightful of a full story, we will leave behind the kingdoms. No longer is it necessary to discuss the battle between King Gregory and King Damon. It has come to the point in our new born story to take a turn, leaving behind what no longer holds importance. For by the very nature of any tale of a fine story, twists are essential for defining the very class from which a fine story is born into. We leave with the tale what belongs to the tale and continue with what belongs to our story. And a fine story it will prove to be, indeed.

At this point in our tale, my devoted listener, your intrigue and curiosity persist to know what transpired in our tale of Gregory, Damon and the kingdoms. But I assure you all is well and good, for we didn't start our tale with the traditional and most common of beginnings. As we've determined, it would render our tale dull and lacking any luster. And to have begun at the middle point would have degraded our fine story to be, leaving out pertinent information. It was somewhere between the traditional beginning and middle age of our tale, birthing a fine story from which we began. And as most people are aware and is customary, in the spirit of our beginning, we find that the middle does not focus on what has happened before. It, too, becomes no longer of an importance worth mentioning. Rather, it relinquishes itself to the duty of becoming a marker, pinpointing a locale of origin pertaining to our tale that has now reached its midlife, which transforms our tale to a full-fledged story of refine. Yes, a twist is now in order to make our story to be of proper class. Let us explore what is around this most intriguing corner in this fine tale of a story.

A Tale of a Story: Crossroads

We left off with two kingdoms opposed. One was about to wage war unbeknownst to the other. Which kingdom is which, and to which ruler belongs where is of no importance at this crucial point in time. What is important is the timing of the precepts of the war to be waged. Such precepts are instilled in all great and proper stories, building cause for the actions to be. And war demands the attention of any listener. For our intent and purposes, war it is. Our characters are mere ornaments to the underlying machine at work. For no visible entity is without an underlying machine driving the force that moves a fine story along. Stories immemorial have proven this to be a precise fact.

What is the point of all this? You may ask. I'll tell you the point of all that has manifested thus far, and shortly to conclude. In order to have a story of a fine class, you must build the interest of the listener. Cast a bait hook, for an empty hook seldom reels any takers in. You must bait the hook, as with any kind of fishing. Except when a net is cast, of course. Should you, my dear and most beloved listener, still be under the influence of confusion, blame not this fine story before you. For it is a fine story, indeed! If you have come this far with me along the journey of this wondrous story, then with these last few words, I will prove to you of the fine and proper class this story claims to be and show you I, as a storyteller, have fulfilled all my obligations and more in creating a fine and proper story. As a storyteller, I have created and piqued an interest within the listener. I have provided precepts to bring us to our current placement within. I have created an unusual twist that makes this story utterly unique, unlike any other. This extraordinary ending has reeled you in and intrigued you . I have brought you to this final and main point of any story. The end cares not the means. I truly hope you have enjoyed this extraordinarily unusual adventure, a tale of a story.

Dream Escape

It all starts with a dream. Dreams... Dreams are raw and unformed foundations. On their own, they bear no weight. But if we nurture them, guide them, coax them into manifesting themselves in our reality, dreams become wonders of amazement surpassed only by love. Nothing in the universe, or in existence, gives one such an explosive emotional experience (except for love), as do dreams the moment they manifest themselves into reality. And there's definitely times when witnessing a dream being born, it's nearly impossible to distinguish one from the other. Love. Dreams. Dreams. Love. Often, they become one and the same.

Fifty-Four, Soon to Be Fifty-Five

Fifty-four, soon to be fifty-five.
Thirty more years I have survived.
Children matured and on their own.
I'm still living without a proper home.
Youth fading as time goes past.
Too many years sitting on my ass.
Ex-wife in and out of our lives.
Spoke of love and brighter skies.
I kick the ground and curse the stars,
Complaining the distance to my car.
I left the jungles far behind.
I'm fifty-four, soon to be fifty-five.

Exit Stage Left

As I conclude this collection of poems and tidbits (new and old) for your entertainment, and exit stage left. I implore you to try and keep your dreams alive as long as it takes to make them a reality. I can only hope you have enjoyed reading this sampling of my creations. Thank you for allowing my humble words to be a part of your day! May peace be in every aspect of your life.

Best Wishes,
D. C. Turner

www.ingramcontent.com/pod-product-compliance
Lightning Source LLC
Chambersburg PA
CBHW031412040426
42444CB00005B/535